GW00400261

Content

Chicken cheeseburger

Turkey pan

Stuffed squash

Bean Salad

Puff pastry with feta cheese

Mushrooms pan

Turkey Breast Wraps

Cream of paprika and tomato soup

Herb soup with egg

Waffles

Donuts

Almond Cookies

Chia Pudding

Powerball

Sweet balls

Chocolate pralines

Cinnamon Balls

Stuffed figs

Honey curd

Peanut Crepes

Spinach Omelet

Curd Fruit

Banana Dessert in a Jar

Chickpea fritters

Introduction

Why are students so reluctant to cook? If you ask them, you often get answers like this: no money, no time or no desire. Or all at once. Most of the time, their menu consists of canned food, cafeteria food, ready-made pizza or burgers.

 But this is not such a good idea, dear students! You should really know: without a balanced, energy-rich meal with lots of fresh ingredients, it's hard to study because the power for the synapses is missing.

Now the excuses are finally over. With this cookbook, it will no longer be a problem to cook for yourself and conjure up 5-star course menus. Promise ;)   In this cookbook you will neither get to know very complicated, nor very expensive recipes. Ah yes, you don't need any cooking experience either! So what are you waiting for? Quickly continue to browse!   I hope you enjoy reading and testing the recipes.

Muesli with fruits

Duration: 20 minutes

Servings: For one person

Ingredients:

- 30g protein powder, flavor of your choice

- 3 tablespoons low-fat quark

- 4 tablespoons water

- 1 tsp psyllium husks

- ½ vanilla pod

- 2 tbsp walnut kernels, chopped

- 1 tbsp. soy flakes

- ½ kiwi

- ¼ apple

- 3 strawberries

How to make:

1. Peel kiwis, cut into slices and quarter each slice again. Wash strawberries, remove stalk and cut into quarters. Wash and core apple and cut into small cubes.
2. Put curd, water, psyllium, vanilla and flakes in a bowl and mix well. Then chill the finished mixture for 15 minutes.
3. Add the chopped walnuts and fruit and mix well again. And your fruit muesli is ready!

Calories: 450 kcal

Protein: 42g

Carbohydrates: 15g

Fat: 22g

Amranth - Raspberry - Layers

Duration: 10 minutes

Servings: For one person

Ingredients:

- 40 g of popped amaranth

- 100 g raspberries, fresh or frozen

- 1 pinch of cinnamon

- 100 ml milk

- Fresh mint leaves

How to make it:

1. Puree half of the amaranth together with raspberries, cinnamon and milk. Pour part of the finished mixture into a glass.
2. As a second layer, add some of the popped amaranth. Continue layering in this way until the glass is completely filled.
3. Finally, garnish with a few raspberries and fresh mint.

Calories: 200 kcal

Protein: 7g

Carbohydrates: 30g

Fat: 5g

Pancakes

Duration: 20 minutes

Servings: Serves one

Ingredients:

2 eggs

1 ripe banana

1 pinch of cinnamon

½ tablespoon coconut oil

½ handful fresh berries, agave syrup to sweeten if desired

How to make it:

1. Beat the eggs into a key, coarsely chop the banana and add it to the egg mixture along with the cinnamon.
2. To make a creamy pancake mixture, blend all ingredients with a hand mixer until smooth.
3. In a frying pan, heat the oil on medium heat and use a spoon to form pancakes from the batter. Now bake for about 2-3 minutes until they are golden brown and can be removed from the pan.

4. Flip the pancakes and brown the second side as well. Lift the pancakes out of the pan and stack them into a pancake stack, the typical pancake tower.
5. To serve, garnish with fresh berries and sweeten with agave syrup to taste.

Calories: 200 kcal

Protein: 15g

Carbohydrates: 10g

Fat: 10g

Porridge

Duration: 10 minutes

Servings: For one person

Ingredients:

40 g oatmeal

120 ml hot water or milk

1 handful of berries

1 tsp agave syrup ½ banana

How to make it:

1. Put the oatmeal in a pot and then simmer over medium heat for about 5 minutes.
2. Once the porridge has taken on a creamy porridge form, remove the pot from the stove.
3. Arrange the porridge in a bowl and garnish with toppings as desired.

Calories: 220 kcal

Protein: 5g

Carbohydrates: 40g

Fat: 3g

Scrambled eggs with smoked salmon

Duration: 20 minutes

Servings: For one person

Ingredients:

3 eggs

1 ½ tablespoons milk

1 slice smoked salmon

2 teaspoons chives

1 teaspoon oil

Salt and pepper

How to make it:

1. whisk together eggs, milk, salt and pepper. Cut the chives into fine rolls and the salmon into strips.
2. Put the oil in a hot pan, add the eggs and let them set. Spread the salmon cut into strips on the eggs and let them cook together for a short time.

3. Before serving, sprinkle with the chive rolls.

   Calories: 380 kcal
   Protein: 30g
   Carbohydrates: 4g
   Fat: 25g

Pizza omelet with tuna

Duration: 25 minutes

Servings: For one person

Ingredients:

2 eggs

½ can tuna

½ onion

50 g Gouda, grated

3 tbsp strained tomatoes

2 tbsp milk

1 tbsp oil

salt and pepper

oregano

How to make it:

1. Beat the eggs with milk, salt and pepper. Drain the tuna. Cut the onion into fine strips. Season the strained tomatoes with salt and pepper. 2.
2. Heat oil in a frying pan, pour in the egg mixture and let it set slightly. If the mixture is already fairly firm, spread the strained tomatoes on top. Top with tuna and onions, sprinkle with the grated cheese and oregano and finish cooking until the desired consistency is reached and the cheese has melted.
3. Transfer to a plate and serve.

Calories: 550 kcal
Protein: 50g
Carbohydrates: 10g
Fat: 35g

Crepes

Duration: 25 minutes

Servings: For one

Ingredients:

3 eggs

25 g protein powder, flavor to taste

15 g peanut oil

Water

How to make it:

1. Beat the eggs with the protein powder to form a creamy batter. Add enough water to the batter to make a dough mixture. 2.
2. Add some peanut oil to the pan and spread evenly (e.g. with a piece of kitchen roll). Add about 2 tablespoons of batter at a time to the pan until the crepes are golden brown.

Calories: 400 kcal
Protein: 30g
Carbohydrates: 2g
Fat: 30g

Fitness muesli

Duration: 10 minutes

Servings: For one person

Ingredients:

300g yogurt

50g oatmeal

Walnuts, 2 handfuls

1 apple

1 banana

2 tsp honey

How to make it:

1. Finely grate the apple. Cut banana into thin slices. 2
2. Add remaining ingredients to fruit pieces and mix everything together well in a bowl.
3. Add honey to taste and mix well.

Calories: 650 kcal

Protein: 30g

arbohydrates: 70g

Fat: 25g

Scrambled eggs

Duration: 20 minutes

Servings: For one person

Ingredients:

70g tomatoes

½ onion

½ mozzarella

2 eggs

2 tablespoons milk

2 basil leaves

1 tablespoon canola

oil

Salt and pepper.

How to make it:

1. Combine eggs, milk, salt and pepper in a bowl.

2. Wash and dice the tomatoes. Cut onion into fine rings. Finely chop basil. 3.
3. Add tomatoes, mozzarella and onion to egg mixture and whisk together.
4. Heat oil in a pan and slowly pour egg mixture into pan. Stir until set.
5. Garnish scrambled eggs with basil and serve.

Calories: 430 kcal

Protein: 25g

Carbohydrates: 10g

Fat: 30g

Cheese Omelet

Duration: 20 minutes

Servings: For one person

Ingredients:

2 eggs

½ zucchini

25g edam

2 tbsp milk

½ parsley, chopped

1 tbsp oil

Salt and pepper

How to make it:

1. whisk together eggs, milk, parsley, salt and pepper.
2. Wash zucchini, end remove and cut into fine strips.
3. Heat oil in a pan and add zucchini. Fry until the zucchini strips turn golden brown.

4. Add the egg mixture, sprinkle with cheese and let it set. Turn the omelet several times.

Calories: 630 kcal

Protein: 35g

Carbohydrates: 7g

Fat: 50g

Radishes with resin cheese

Duration: 25 minutes

Servings: Serves one

Ingredients:

40 g resin cheese

½ bunch radishes

½ frisee lettuce

¼ cucumber

½ red onion

1 tbsp sprouts

1 ½ tbsp light balsamic vinegar

1 tbsp vegetable stock.

1 tablespoon olive oil

Salt and pepper

How to make it:

1. Wash the radishes, dry them and slice them thinly.
2. Peel the cucumber and cut into slices. 3.
3. Wash lettuce, spin dry and pick into bite-sized pieces.
4. Peel onion, cut in half and slice thinly, pick apart to make fine rings. 5.
5. Wash the sprouts and spin dry.
6. Chop pickles into fine cubes. Cut cheese into cubes.
7. For the dressing, add vegetable broth, vinegar, olive oil, salt and pepper to a salad bowl and whisk together.
8. Mix all ingredients together except for the frisée lettuce and add to the dressing.
9. Let everything sit together for at least 10 minutes.
10. Season with salt and pepper as needed.
11. Mix the frisee salad with the dressing on plates and serve immediately.

Calories: 180 kcal
Protein: 20g
Carbohydrates: 5g
Fat: 10g

Fish cakes

Duration: 30 minutes

Servings: For one person

Ingredients:

170 g pollock fillet

70 g yogurt

½ egg

1 tomato

½ orange

½ clove garlic

¼ organic lime

1 tsp olive

oil

salt and pepper

1 pinch chili flakes

½ bunch basil

½ tsp mustard

½ tsp canola oil

How to make it:

1. rinse the fresh pollock fillet, pat dry well and finely dice. Then chill in the freezer for about 10 minutes. If frozen fish fillet is used, it should be thawed and then finely diced as well.
2. Peel the orange generously to remove the white skin as well. Fillet the oranges over a bowl to catch the juice. Then finely dice the orange fillets.
3. Wash the tomatoes, remove the stalk and finely dice them as well.
4. Peel and finely chop the garlic. Squeeze the lime and mix the lime juice with the diced tomatoes, oranges and half of the garlic in a bowl.
5. Then season with a teaspoon of olive oil, the chili flakes, salt and pepper.
6. Wash the basil, pat dry, pluck off the leaves and chop finely. Add to another bowl with the remaining garlic, yogurt and olive oil, mix well. Season with salt and pepper to taste.
7. Now remove the fish fillet from the freezer again and chop well in a blender. Separate the egg yolk and egg white, fold the yolk into the fish mixture. Add salt and pepper to taste.

8. Heat a coated frying pan with some canola oil on medium heat. Form flat patties from the fish mixture and fry on both sides for a few minutes. 9.
9. Arrange the fish cakes with the fruity salad and the dip on a plate and serve.

Calories: 320 kcal
Protein: 40g
Carbohydrates: 15g
Fat: 10g

Spaghetti

Duration: 30 minutes

Servings: For one person

Ingredients:

100g spaghetti

125g broccoli

25g butter

25g olives, pitted

¼ lemon

2 tomatoes, dried in oil

½ clove garlic basil

salt and pepper

How to make it:
1. cook spaghetti according to instructions and drain.
2. Cook broccoli in salted water and drain.
3. Squeeze lemon, mix zest with juice and butter.
4. Add basil and season. Meanwhile, preheat the oven to 180 degrees.

5. Cut tomatoes into strips. Cut garlic into slices.
6. Put spaghetti with broccoli, tomatoes and garlic in a baking dish.
7. Add lemon butter, season and mix well.
8. Place casserole dish in oven for 10 minutes and then serve.

Calories: 580 kcal
Protein: 10g
Carbohydrates: 80g
Fat: 25

Spaetzle

Duration: 30 minutes

Servings: For one person

Ingredients:

100g spaetzle

75g Emmental

70g mushrooms

2 tbsp oil

½ leek ½ onion

salt and pepper

How to make it:

1. preheat oven to 200 degrees.
2. Cut leeks into rings. Cut mushrooms in half. Grate cheese.
3. Cook spaetzle according to instructions and drain.
4. Sauté leeks and mushrooms in a pan with oil and after a few minutes add spaetzle and mix well. 5.

5. Place spaetzle mixture and cheese alternately in a baking dish and place in oven.
6. Dice onions and fry in pan with oil.
7. Serve spaetzle, add onions and season with salt and pepper.

Calories: 530 kcal
Protein: 20g
Carbohydrates: 80g
Fat: 20g

Gnocchi

Duration: 20 minutes

Servings: For one person

Ingredients:

200g gnocchi

75g mushrooms

60g spinach leaves

60g blue cheese

50g cream

25ml milk

½ clove garlic

2 tsp butter

2 tsp cider vinegar

salt and pepper

How to make it:

1. heat spinach, milk and cream in a pot. Squeeze garlic into it.
2. Sauté mushrooms in a pan with 1 tsp butter, season and add to spinach.
3. Fry gnocchi in the same pan with butter.
4. Add cheese and vinegar to spinach and season. Then serve.

Calories: 600 kcal
Protein: 5g
Carbohydrates: 90g
Fat: 20g

Chicken fillet

Duration: 30 minutes

Servings: For one person

Ingredients:

130 g zucchini

2 pickled artichoke hearts

1 chicken breast fillets, 170 g

60 ml chicken broth

1 style basil

1 tsp oil

salt and pepper

How to make it:

1. Preheat the oven to 220 °.
2. Wash the zucchini, slice lengthwise with a vegetable slicer, salt a little and set aside.
3. Quarter the drained artichokes, cut the tomatoes into thin strips.
4. Wash the meat and dry it with kitchen paper.

5. Cut 2 pieces of aluminum foil to 30 cm square and brush with 1 tsp oil.
6. Lay out the zucchini on it in the center. Top with the meat and sprinkle with salt and pepper.
7. Distribute the artichokes and tomatoes in the packets and season again if necessary.
8. Fold up the aluminum foil on all sides and press the corners together to form parcels. Leave a little open at the top.
9. Pour the broth into the packets and now close them.
10. Bake the foil packets in the oven on a baking sheet for about 25 minutes.
11. Wash the basil, dry it with a paper towel and roughly pluck apart or roughly chop the leaves.
12. Remove the finished aluminum packets from the oven, and place each on a plate.
13. Serve sprinkled with basil.

Calories: 300 kcal
Protein: 45g
Carbohydrates: 10g
Fat: 5g

Salmon Salad

Duration: 20 minutes

Servings: Serves one

Ingredients:

2 slices smoked salmon, 20 g each

1 egg, boiled

½ cucumber

3 radishes

½ bunch dill

1 tbsp light balsamic vinegar

1 tbsp olive oil

1 tbsp yogurt

½ tsp mustard

Salt and pepper

How to make it:

1. Peel eggs and cut into slices. 2.
2. Peel cucumber, wash radishes and slice both thinly with a vegetable slicer.
3. Wash dill, pat dry and chop finely.
4. For the dressing, whisk together yogurt, vinegar, oil, mustard, salt, pepper and dill.
5. Arrange salmon slices on plates, top with egg slices, add radishes and cucumber slices and drizzle dressing over.

Calories: 260 kcal
Protein: 15g
Carbohydrates: 5g
Fat: 20g

Shrimp vegetable skillet

Duration: 20 minutes

Servings: For one serving

Ingredients:

5 organic headless shrimp

½ red bell bell pepper

½ red yellow bell bell pepper

1 zucchini

2 mushrooms

3 cherry tomatoes

2 sprigs of rosemary

1 sprig of thyme Olive oil

1 clove of garlic

½ lemon, juice

Salt and pepper

How to make it:

1. first peel and chop the garlic, then mix it in a bowl with a tablespoon of olive oil and salt and pepper. 2
2. Remove the shell of the shrimp and pull the intestines. Then roll the shrimp in the oil mixture and let them sit.
3. Wash the zucchini, cut off the ends, quarter lengthwise and cut into small pieces. Clean the peppers and mushrooms as well. Remove the seeds from the peppers and chop them into small cubes, as well as the mushrooms. Also wash the cherry tomatoes, pat dry and cut into quarters. Chop the rosemary together with the garlic.
4. Now put a pan with some oil on the stove on high heat. Sauté the zucchini first, then add the rest of the vegetables with the garlic, rosemary and thyme and sauté. Season with salt and pepper to taste. Then remove the vegetables from the pan and set aside.
5. Next, sauté the shrimp in the pan and add a little lemon juice. Arrange the shrimp and vegetables on a plate and serve.

Calories: 230 kcal
Protein: 25g
Carbohydrates: 10g
Fat: 10g

Zucchini pizza

Duration: 30 minutes

Servings: For 1 pizza

Ingredients:

1 zucchini

1 egg

50 g spelt flour

4 mushrooms

Herb salt

Arugula Eggplant

1 can of strained tomatoes

How to make it:

1. wash the zucchini and grate it with a grater. The zucchini will be very watery, but try to pat it dry as best you can with a paper towel.
2. This step is very crucial to make the pizza nice and crispy. To the grated zucchini, add an egg and 50g of spelt flour and mix to form a dough.

3. Season the mixture with Italian herb salt. Now heat some oil in a pan and pour the zucchini batter into the pan. Fry both sides until golden brown.
4. Meanwhile, preheat the oven to 200 degrees (top and bottom heat) and start preparing the ingredients for the topping of the pizza. Cut and wash the mushrooms, eggplant, arugula and ham.
5. Feel free to vary with the vegetables. After the zucchini base is baked crispy, remove it from the pan and brush it with the strained tomatoes.
6. Then place all the ingredients for the topping on the pizza and put it in the oven for about 5 to 10 minutes. Depending on the degree of browning, remove the pizza from the oven. Enjoy your meal.

Calories: 550 kcal
Protein: 5g
Carbohydrates: 80g
Fat: 15g

Tortellini Salad

Duration: 15 minutes

Servings: For one person

Ingredients:

100g tortellini

50g mozzarella

25g olives

30g arugula

½ bell pepper

1 tbsp vinegar

2 tbsp oil

2 tsp herbs, mixed

Salt and pepper

How to make it:

1. cook tortellini according to instructions and drain.
2. Combine herb mixture, vinegar and oil in a bowl, season and whisk together.
3. Pluck arugula. Dice bell bell pepper.

4. Pit olives and chop finely.
5. Add all remaining ingredients to bowl, season and mix properly.
6. Serve tortellini salad immediately.

Calories: 600 kcal
Protein: 10g
Carbohydrates: 80g
Fat: 25g

Chicken breast fillet with fried egg

Duration: 15 minutes

Servings: For one serving

Ingredients:

3 eggs

250 g chicken breast fillet

1 tomato

How to make it:

1. Heat some oil in a pan and meanwhile chop the tomato. Also cut the chicken fillet into 3 flat slices.
2. Now add the fillet to the pan and sear it for a few minutes on both sides. After that, prepare the fried eggs in another pan. prepare the fried eggs in another pan.
3. Place the fillet pieces on a plate, place the tomato slices on top and layer a fried egg on each fillet piece. Finally, season the dish with salt and pepper. This is a great dish that only takes 15 minutes to make.

Calories: 550 kcal
Protein: 80g
Carbohydrates: 5g
Fat: 25g

Chicken cheeseburger

Duration: 30 minutes

Servings: For one person

Ingredients:

300 g chicken breast fillets

5 lettuce leaves

2 tbsp natural yogurt

1 red onion

salt and pepper

1 tomato

2 slices Gouda herbs

2 tsp tomato paste

How to make it:

1. chop the chicken meat and mix it with some of the red onion and spices. Now form an oval burger out of the chopped chicken meat and fry it.

2. Once the meat is cooked through, place the onion rings, tomato slices and cheese on top. Put a lid on the pan so the cheese melts.
3. Now place the lettuce leaves on a plate. Also, mix a sauce of 2 tablespoons of plain yogurt and some tomato paste and spread it on the lettuce leaves.
4. Finally, place the burger on top. The low carb burger, low carb burger where you will not miss the bread.

Calories: 250 kcal
Protein: 40g
Carbohydrates: 5g
Fat: 7

Turkey pan

Duration: 20 minutes

Servings: For one person

Ingredients:

½ feta cheese

½ can mushrooms

250 g turkey cutlets

1 tbsp ajvar

2 tbsp olive oil

basil

How to make it:

1. heat plenty of olive oil in a pan and add the turkey cutlets. Sear it on all sides and reduce the heat of the stovetop.

2. Now add the mushrooms. If they are too big, slice them first. Crumble the feta cheese, add it to the pan and let it melt completely. melt.
3. Then stir in the ajvar and season with salt and pepper. Once you have served the dish, add some fresh basil on top. Very easy and quick to prepare, a real treat.

Calories: 450 kcal
Protein: 70g
Carbohydrates: 1g
Fat: 20g

Stuffed squash

Duration: 30 minutes

Servings: For one person

Ingredients:

½ Hokkaido 150 g minced meat

70 g tomatoes

½ yellow bell pepper

50 g mushrooms

100 g cottage cheese

25 g feta

½ onion olive oil

salt and pepper

paprika powder

rosemary

thyme

How to make it:

1. first preheat the oven to 180 degrees, cut the pumpkin in half and remove the seeds. Wash and chop the tomatoes, peppers and mushrooms. Chop the spices, cut the feta cheese into small cubes or crumble with your fingers.
2. In a pan, sweat the onions with a little oil and brown the minced meat. Season with salt and pepper.
3. Then add the vegetables to the pan and fry everything together until the vegetables become a little soft.
4. Then add the cottage cheese, mix everything well and season, also add the fresh herbs.
5. fill the mixture into the pumpkin halves and sprinkle the feta cubes on top. Put the pumpkin halves on a baking tray (if they are not standing properly, help them out with crumpled baking paper). Then cook in the oven for about 25 minutes.
6. Test with a knife if the flesh of the pumpkin is cooked.

Calories: 670 kcal

Protein: 50g

Carbohydrates: 40g

Fat: 30g

Bean Salad

Duration: 20 minutes

Servings: For one person

Ingredients:

400 g white beans

1 red bell pepper

½ cucumber

½ red onion

olive oil

herbs

salt and bell pepper

How to make it:

1. cut the onion, bell pepper and cucumber into rough pieces and chop the herbs. Now wash the beans and drain them well.
2. Then put all the ingredients in a salad bowl and mix it all together with some salt and pepper. Finally,

add red wine dressing or olive oil olive oil to the salad. If you like it a bit spicier, feel free to chop a hot pepper and add it.

Calories: 280 kcal
Protein: 25g
Carbohydrates: 30g
Fat: 2g

Puff pastry with feta cheese

Duration: 25 minutes

Servings: For one person

Ingredients:

150g puff pastry

50g feta cheese

1 egg

½ leek

25ml vegetable broth

50g cocktail tomatoes

4 hot peppers

1 tsp oil

Salt and pepper

How to make it:

1. cut leeks into rings and sauté in a pan with oil.
2. Add vegetable broth and let it boil.
3. Preheat oven to 220 degrees.

4. Cut tomatoes in half. Crumble the feta cheese and add to the pan with the egg and season.
5. Spread puff pastry on a baking sheet lined with baking paper.
6. Spread pan mixture on puff pastry. Put tomatoes and peppers on top.
7. Then place baking sheet in preheated oven for 10 minutes.
8. Wrap in aluminum foil and serve immediately.

Calories: 700 kcal
Protein: 20g
Carbohydrates: 100g
Fat: 30g

Mushrooms pan

Duration: 25 minutes

Servings: For one person

Ingredients:

100 g mushrooms

100 g cherry tomatoes

50 g arugula

80 g cream cheese

Salt and pepper

How to make it:

1. wash and quarter the mushrooms. Wash and chop tomatoes. Wash arugula.
2. Fry mushrooms in hot oil. Add tomatoes and cream cheese. Simmer for five minutes. Add arugula and cook briefly. Season with salt and pepper.

Calories: 220 kcal
Protein: 10g
Carbohydrates: 10g
Fat: 15g

Turkey Breast Wraps

Duration: 20 minutes

Servings: For one person

Ingredients:

2 slices turkey breast

2 leaves iceberg lettuce

½ bell pepper

2 tbsp flour

1 tbsp peanut butter

40ml water

pinch of salt

How to make it:

1. put flour, salt and water in bowl, mix and knead.
2. Finely chop bell pepper and lettuce leaves.
3. Roll out dough and bake in pan for 2 minutes on both sides.
4. Remove patties and spread with peanut butter.

5. Spread turkey breast, lettuce and bell bell pepper and roll.

Calories: 370 kcal

Protein: 30g

Carbohydrates: 10g

Fat: 15g

Cream of paprika and tomato soup

Duration: 30 minutes

Servings: Serves one

Ingredients:

1 shallot

½ tablespoon olive oil

200 ml vegetable broth

½ red bell bell pepper

½ yellow bell bell pepper

2 tomatoes

½ tablespoon tomato paste

½ tablespoon creme fraiche

thyme

cilantro

cayenne pepper

chili powder

salt and pepper

How to make it:

1. preheat your oven to 200 degrees (convection).
   Now wash the red bell bell pepper and the
   tomatoes. Roughly quarter the peppers and score
   the tomatoes crosswise on the underside.
2. Then place the diced peppers and tomatoes on a
   baking sheet lined with parchment paper and bake
   for 10 minutes. Now put on a classic vegetable
   broth.
3. Next, peel the shallots and cut them into rings. Now
   peel off the skin of the baked tomatoes and
   peppers and cut the flesh into pieces.
4. Now heat the oil in a pot and sweat the shallots.
   Then add the bell pepper and tomato pieces and let
   it simmer for about 3 minutes. Now add the
   vegetable broth and tomato paste and puree with a
   hand blender.
5. Now season the soup with chili, paprika, cayenne
   bell pepper, coriander and a little salt while the
   soup simmers on low heat for about 5 minutes.
6. Now wash and cut the peppers into very small
   cubes and add the cubes to the soup along with the
   créme fraiche. Let it simmer for another 10
   minutes. Sprinkle a few thyme leaves over the soup
   before serving.

Calories: 150 kcal

Protein: 5g

Carbohydrates: 20g

Fat: 5g

Herb soup with egg

Duration: 30 minutes

Servings: For one person

Ingredients:

25 g wild garlic

25 g nettle

25 g watercress

50 g spinach

1 tbsp cress

1 tbsp parsley

½ tbsp dill

½ spring onion

300 ml vegetable broth

25 ml cream

½ tbsp butter

1 egg, boiled

Salt and pepper

Nutmeg

How to make it:

1. wash the herbs, drain well and then chop finely. Clean the spring onion, wash and cut into fine rings.
2. Melt the butter in a saucepan, add the spring onions and sauté. Add the herbs and deglaze with the broth. Bring to the boil briefly and season with salt, pepper and nutmeg.
3. Peel the hard-boiled egg and cut into slices.
4. Stir the cream into the soup, boil again briefly, pour into a plate and spread the egg slices on top.

Calories: 280 kcal
Protein: 10g
Carbohydrates: 5g
Fat: 20g

Waffles

Duration: 20 minutes

Servings: For one person

Ingredients:

25 g butter

50 g curd

2 eggs

3 tbsp protein powder

1 tbsp oil

Xucker

How to make it:

1. beat the eggs in a bowl until foamy. Then add the butter and stir everything well.
2. Now add 1 tablespoon of oil and the quark and stir all ingredients well.
3. Now add the egg white powder and mix everything through.
4. Now preheat your waffle iron and grease it.

5. Now pour some batter into the waffle iron and bake the waffle.

Calories: 360 kcal

Protein: 25g

Carbohydrates: 2g

Fat: 33g

Donuts

Duration: 30 minutes

Servings: 8 donuts

Ingredients:

100 xylitol

60 g protein powder

60 g almonds, ground

3 eggs

2 tablespoons cocoa powder

2 tablespoons butter

2 tablespoons sour cream

1 teaspoon vanilla flavoring

¼ teaspoon salt

¼ teaspoon baking powder

 ¼ teaspoon cinnamon

How to make it:

1. Separate eggs and beat the whites to egg whites.
2. Melt butter and let cool briefly.
3. Add xylitol and butter to egg yolks and beat until fluffy.
4. Carefully fold the beaten egg whites into the egg yolk mixture.
5. Gradually add the ground almonds, cocoa powder, vanilla flavoring, salt, baking powder and cinnamon.
6. Stir until an even batter is formed.
7. Pour the dough into donut molds.
8. Bake at 175 ° C for 15 minutes.
9. In the meantime, mix the protein powder with the sour cream.
10. Let donuts cool slightly and spread with frosting.

Per donut
Calories: 150 kcal
Protein: 8g
Carbohydrates: 5g
Fat: 14g

Almond Cookies

Duration: 20 minutes

Servings: 20 cookies

Ingredients:

250 g almond butter

220 g butter

200 g egg white powder

30 ml water

25 g sugar

20 almonds, peeled

1 egg

1 teaspoon vanilla flavoring

½ teaspoon salt

½ teaspoon baking powder

How to make it:

1. Cream the butter with the sugar.

2. Gradually add the egg, almond butter, salt, baking powder and vanilla flavoring. Then fold in the protein powder and add water.
3. Stir until a uniform dough is formed.
4. Form 30 cookies with wet hands. Spread on a baking sheet lined with parchment paper. Place an almond in the center of each cookie. Bake at 190 degrees for 10 minutes.

Per cookie Calories: 160 kcal
Protein: 10g
Carbohydrates: 7g
Fat: 7g

Chia Pudding

Duration: 20 minutes

Servings: For one person

Ingredients:

3 tbsp chia seeds

250ml almond milk cinnamon powder

2 tbsp agave syrup

½ mango

100g strawberries

How to make it:

1. puree chia seeds with 70ml almond milk and cinnamon.
2. Stir in 180ml almond milk with agave syrup.
3. Leave in the fridge for an hour, stirring occasionally, until you have a creamy pudding.
4. Peel and finely chop the mango. Finely chop berries.
5. Garnish pudding with fruit and then serve.

Calories: 170 kcal
Protein: 10g
Carbohydrates: 25g
Fat: 2g

Powerball

Duration: 30 minutes

Servings: 30 balls

Ingredients:

70 g cashews

30 g rolled oats

20 g pumpkin seeds

10 g sunflower seeds

200 g dates

180 g cranberries

Popped amaranth for rolling

How to make it:

1. Pour boiling water over the cashews and let soak for a few minutes.
2. Grind the oat flakes, pumpkin seeds and sunflower seeds into flour using a food processor.
3. Now grind the drained cashews together with the dates and cranberries in a food processor.

4. Now combine the two doughs and knead well.
5. Sprinkle the popped amaranth on a plate, form balls with the dough and roll them in the pops. Place the powerballs in the refrigerator.

Per ball
Calories: 50 kcal
Protein: 1g
Carbohydrates: 4g
Fat: 3g

Sweet balls

Duration: 10 minutes

Servings: 15 balls

Ingredients:

12 tbsp. quinoa or millet

150 g dates

2 tbsp. pressed orange juice

2 tbsp. cashews, grated

2 tbsp. tiger nut puree

 3 tbsp. agave syrup

1 tsp. cinnamon powder

Unsweetened cocoa powder

How to make it:

1. Put all the ingredients in a bowl and mix to a homogeneous mass. Shape into balls with wet hands and coat in cocoa powder.

Per ball

Calories: 80 kcal

Protein: 2g

Carbohydrates: 13g

Fat: 2g

Chocolate pralines

Duration: 15 minutes / 60 minutes in the refrigerator

Servings: 12 balls

Ingredients:

100 g of edible curd

100 g of cream cheese

1 tbsp coconut oil

2 tbsp almond oil

½ tsp vanilla powder

1 tsp xylitol

12 raspberries

1 bar dark chocolate

How to make it:

1. Mix the edible curd, coconut oil, flour, vanilla, cream cheese and xylitol in a bowl until well combined.

2. Form small balls from the resulting mixture and put a raspberry in each ball.
3. Melt the dark chocolate in a water bath. Then cover the balls with the chocolate and place in the refrigerator for an hour.

Per chocolate
Calories: 80 kcal
Protein: 3g
Carbohydrates: 7g
Fat: 6g

Cinnamon Balls

Duration: 25 minutes

Servings: 10 balls

Ingredients:

250 g pecans

½ tsp cinnamon

10 dates, pitted

½ tsp sea salt

How to make it:

1. Preheat the oven to 180 ° and line a baking tray with baking paper. Soak the dates in warm water for 15 minutes and then drain.
2. Then knead all the ingredients into a dough and use it to form small balls. Then spread these balls on the baking sheet and bake in the oven for about 10 minutes.

Per ball

Calories: 200 kcal

Protein: 2g

Carbohydrates: 18g

Fat: 6g

Stuffed figs

Duration: 10 minutes

Servings: For one person

Ingredients:

2 figs ½ hazelnut kernels, ground

50 g of cottage cheese

¼ organic lemon

Black pepper

How to make it:

1. wash figs and cut off one lid at a time. Now carefully scoop out the pulp.
2. Mix the pulp, nuts and curd in a bowl until well blended.
3. Squeeze half of the lemon and season the mixture with pepper.
4. Finally, put the filling in the figs and enjoy.

Calories: 400 kcal

Protein: 15g

Carbohydrates: 20g

Fat: 25g

Honey curd

Duration: 5 minutes

Servings: For one person

Ingredients:

100 g of cottage cheese

20 ml of milk

1 tsp of honey

How to make it:

put all the ingredients in a bowl and mix everything together well.

Calories: 110 kcal

Protein: 12g

Carbohydrates: 12g

Fat: 1g

Peanut Crepes

Duration: 25 minutes

Servings: For one

Ingredients:

3 eggs

20 g protein powder, flavor to taste

15 g peanut oil

Water

How to make it:

1. Beat the eggs with the protein powder until a creamy batter is formed. Add enough water to the batter to make a dough mixture.
2. Add some peanut oil to the pan and spread evenly (e.g. with a piece of kitchen roll). Add about 2 tablespoons of batter at a time to the pan until the crepes are golden brown.

Calories: 400 kcal

Protein: 30g

Carbohydrates: 3g

Fat: 27g

Spinach Omelet

Duration: 20 minutes

Servings: For one person

Ingredients:

2 eggs

50g spinach leaves, frozen

Seasoning of choice

How to make it:

1. first defrost the spinach in a suitable dish in the microwave.
2. Meanwhile, crack the eggs into a bowl and whisk until foamy. Then add salt, pepper and other spices to taste.
3. When the spinach is thawed, stir it into the egg.
4. Pour the egg and spinach mixture into a non-stick skillet and cook on high until set, 3-4 minutes. Then turn the omelet over and fry from the other side as well.
5. Finally, lift the omelet out of the pan and serve on a plate.

Calories: 330 kcal
Protein: 30g
Carbohydrates: 5g
Fat: 20g

Curd Fruit

Duration: 10 minutes

Servings: For one person

Ingredients:

1 kiwi

1 handful of raspberries

2 tablespoons of cottage cheese

How to make it:

1. peel the kiwi and cut the flesh into small pieces.
2. Using a hand blender, puree the kiwi and half of the cottage cheese, and in another container, puree the raspberries with the remaining cottage cheese.
3. Alternate 1 tablespoon of both purees in a shot glass.

Calories: 40 kcal

Protein: 3g

Carbohydrates: 5g

Fat: 1g

Banana Dessert in a Jar

Duration: 20 minutes

Servings: For one person

Ingredients:

3 tablespoons plain yogurt

3 tablespoons cream cheese

1 banana

2 ladyfingers

How to make it:

1. stir together cream cheese and yogurt in a bowl.
2. In a tall glass, place a layer of crumbled ladyfingers and top with some cream.
3. Cut a banana into small pieces and put it in the glass as the 3rd layer. Top with the rest of the cream and enjoy directly.

Calories: 230 kcal

Protein: 15g

Carbohydrates: 15g

Fat: 15g

Chickpea fritters

Duration: 20 minutes

Servings: For one person

Ingredients:

100 g chickpeas

25 g onions

½ clove of garlic

½ tsp cumin

How to make it:

1. Peel and cut the onions as well as the garlic clove into small pieces. Then wash the chickpeas and put them in a blender together with the chopped vegetables and cumin and puree everything for 50 seconds on medium speed.
2. Now take the frying mixture, form small balls from it, which you then flatten a bit, and fry them in a pan with a little oil for 5-7 minutes on medium-high heat.
3. The fritters can be combined well with the recipe on page 12.

Calories: 100 kcal
Protein: 5g
Carbohydrates: 12g
Fat: 2g

Imprint
Hans-Dieter Swoboda
Gerbersruhstr. 153
69158 Wiesloch
GERMANY

Printed in Great Britain
by Amazon

39301443R00056